TWEED

Rachelle Mbuangi

1st WORLD
PUBLISHING

TWEED

Rachelle Mbuangi

© Rachelle Mbuangi 2008

Published by 1stWorld Publishing
P.O. Box 2211 Fairfield, Iowa 52556
tel: 641-209-5000 • fax: 641-209-3001
web: www.1stworldpublishing.com

First Edition

LCCN: 2008933552
SoftCover ISBN: 978-1-4218-9007-4
HardCover ISBN: 978-1-4218-9006-7
eBook ISBN: 978-1-4218-9008-1

THE INTRODUCTION

This book is an exhaustive effort to explain the phenomenon of racial divide between Black Americans and Africans and between White Americans and Black Americans. The title of this book, "TWEED," is derived from the nickname of the great Martin Luther King Jr. This book gives many different fact-based theories on racial issues. It also has a strong religious tone. Though the issue of race does raise a great deal of controversy, this book was written in an effort to unravel the cords of mass confusion propagated by many years of hate and apartheid. Hopefully, this book will help soften some of the harshest opinions and help those with no opinion form one. Read this book at your own risk. It does carry the mind off of its present course.

CHAPTER 1:
SMALL CAP OF HISTORY

There is a truth about black, white and racism that some may not be aware exists or may deny its existence. Unsurprisingly, blacks are unaware of this theoretical truth while whites live in denial of it.

Let's start with the first settlers. I would gather the English were attracted to the colonizing efforts by the Spaniards to the south of the mainland, so they came to this land due to the call of exploration. These English colonists "self-discovered" this land, but we know the truth about that, don't we! Respectively, we do have to give tribute where it is due. The settlers did come to this land just as the land was. There was nothing here besides nature and the Native Americans. In their colonizing effort, the settlers did meet many hurdles, and they overcame those obstacles not knowing what would be the end result of their sacrifice.

The settlers had to build their own little civilization from scratch, so they began to build an association with the Native Americans. This eventually turned into bartering and led to the Native Americans embarking on new exchange opportunities with the settlers. The settlers had to drink the same water that they were using as a bathroom, which was nothing more than a nearby river or stream of water. In addition, the newcomers began falling ill from an unknown virus. It had gotten so bad that they began to believe the Indians had attacked them with a biological weapon. However, even if the Indians had a biological weapon—what it would have been made of—poison berries!

The settlers began to retaliate against the same natives who were kind enough to show them how to grow food and kind enough to befriend them. We know the rest; eventually the settlers turned homicidal and slaughtered the Native Americans, taking the land and making it their own. It wasn't until later that they found out the virus that had made them ill was from their very own drinking water. Whether we like it or not, Yahweh allowed this travesty to happen, but I dare not think it will be without consequence.

The first blacks came as slaves to work in agriculture for the settlers while the settlers were busy building and doing the back breaking work of colonizing. Blacks need to understand one thing about the settlers: they were not afraid to die for their bottom line. Likewise, they did not mind taking land that did not belong to them. Regardless, the settlers are the reason why we have the country that we have today, and although we do not have to like it, we do have to bitterly respect it. Somehow, they must have enough skin on their backsides to pay the price for it.

Furthermore, during the American War of Independence there were black soldiers that came with the British who were promised freedom if they helped fight. For the blacks that did fight, their blood was spilled in vain. When the British army came to fight the Americans, the blacks came along with the British knowing this fight was not theirs. As soon as their feet hit American soil, they made a run for it. I do not blame the blacks for running because it was not their land, their fight was for freedom. Eventually, after the Americans won their independence from the British, the whites did what they do best. They tied up the loose ends, "so to speak," by rounding up the escaped blacks, overcoming them, and enslaving them.

That was a small recap of history, but now let's fast forward to the D.C. Emancipation Act signed by President Lincoln. This act ended slavery in the District of Columbia before the initial Emancipation Proclamation. Lincoln did this to end agitation with anti-slavery activist calling it the "national shame" to have had slavery in the nation's capital. The D.C. EA provided immediate emancipation compensation of up to $300 for each slave for loyal unionist masters, voluntary colonization of former slaves to colonies outside the U.S., and payments of up to $100 for persons choosing immigration. The blacks refused to go, however, because they felt like they were Americans too. This decision on the part of the blacks was largely because they were so out of touch with Africa and Israel many, if not the majority of blacks, had no knowledge about Africa or Israel. Unfortunately, due to the decision of the blacks to stay in America, it basically sealed our fate from that point on and led to the slaughter of many blacks in their fight for equal rights.

Now, let me make one point about the initial Emancipation Proclamation. It was issued January 1, 1863, and signed by President Lincoln. This came as the nation approached its third year of civil war. The proclamation declared that "all persons held as slaves within the rebellious states are and henceforth shall be free." Despite the expansive wording, the Emancipation Proclamation was limited.

It applied only to states that had succeeded from the Union, leaving slavery untouched in the loyal border states. It also exempted parts of the Confederacy that had already come under northern control. Most importantly, the freedom it promised depended on Union military victory.

Looking at the future of blacks beyond the Civil War, it is my opinion that Lincoln knew white America would not give these newly freed blacks a chance in society. This eventually led to massive apartheid. In my opinion, blacks have since evolved into a co-dependent mindset. Since the slaves arrived in the America's they were stripped of their true identity and their culture. Henceforth, making it easier for the slave masters to mold the slave into whatever suited him. Christianity was used as a tool to make the "perfect slave" by distorting Holy Scripture to make the blacks docile. Blacks did not want to be too far from their bread and water once they were freed. Blacks became content with white America providing everything they needed, and they didn't mind being, and still don't mind being, the prey of America. In my opinion, only a very few whites nationwide actually don't like blacks simply because of their color. Rather, the patriotic whites of America don't like blacks because of their co-dependent mindsets.

Whites would be elated for us to go pave our own way, just as the early settlers did. At least we don't have to go steal the land. The land already belongs to us; we just need to do something with it. Yahweh gave us Africa; it is ours and we have collectively abandoned her. Being that blacks in America are the true people of Yahweh, we have also abandoned Israel. For starters, the reason I believe so many blacks are closed to the idea of Africa is because of the heavily watered-down documentaries shown of the wild in Africa. Blacks in America believe all of Africa is just jungle, and even for those that know better, they are afraid. Whites intended for ethnocide to happen. That's why they remind us as often as they can who we are. All in the same, if all foreigners saw of the U.S. was its "country" aspects, as opposed to showing its wonderful cities, many immigrants would stay home. Africa is modernized enough for people to love to vacation there and some even have moved from America to Africa and from Africa to Israel.

Whites have been doing missionary work in Africa for decades, while us blacks stand by and watch the white people do for our people, what we should be doing for our people. I can't help but wonder if the African people feel abandoned by black America, and why we are not the ones adopting their children and feeding their starving. I can say one thing: don't blame the white people for our lack of involvement, because if white America could have its way they would send every black person back to Africa whether you want to go or not.

Blacks tend to enjoy sitting under Mr. Whitey's table. We tend to enjoy the crumbs that fall from it, some of us even get whole turkeys and some get chicken legs and some, pot roasts. The blacks that get whole turkeys from Mr. Whitey's table are your wealthiest blacks, and those who get the crumbs are your middle class and poverty blacks. You mean to tell me this is a life for our children to be proud of? It seems blacks of America would rather make their seat under a table rather than build their own table and let Yahweh prepare it. That's what the settlers did, good or bad, right or wrong. They built their table and Yahweh did prepare it and likewise going to destroy it. So, what is our excuse for not being independently productive for our own people?

Here is a basic truth that stands for any man's house: "you cannot go into another person's home and stake your claim."

We as blacks do not have the support of those who built this country to become shareholders of this country. We Hebrews were enslaved in Egypt for 400 years, and many generations' of us were born in Egypt but that never made us Egyptian. Although the success of America as a whole did come from the many immigrants around the world, it has never made those of us of a dark skin color gain any acceptance from the white Americans. We cannot continue on the present course of trying to make Mr. Whitey "like us." We cannot continue trying to make them feel guilty of the past, because they just remind us all the more who we are not. This makes room for us to learn who we really are.

If you don't believe me, look at the Katrina victims. It seems to me, it is better to be a black Katrina victim in Africa than in Utah. I believe the reason we saw so many blacks treated like animals in New Orleans was simply because the government did not want to waste its resources on a people they feel is already a drain on society. Not to mention there is a law that only considers blacks 3/5 of a human; so this law will protect the benefactors when they treat blacks like animals. The government already views blacks as unproductive citizens, so in their minds, it probably would be better for our people to die rather than continuing being a burden on white taxpayers. I also know that there were white people affected by the storm but between the two, who do you believe America feels is more deserving of the help? Blacks in this country have managed to close their eyes to these things so long as they can keep eating from the white man's table. This is an embarrassment to our people, do we have any shame? There is no need to try and kill a weed by cutting off its limbs, you must kill the root.

We have various black factions that believe they are making a difference. These are the ones that eat crumbs from Mr.

Whitey's table and hide the steaks in their pockets. These black factions have missed the point that the great Dr. Martin Luther King died trying to make. We are still trying to live off of his dream. Don't you see black America, we are living his dream. Now it is time for us to move on to a new dream. Martin L. King did not die for us to dry up in his dream or vision. He died so we can have a new one; Martin knew we could not win this kind of battle fighting carnally. That's why before he understood himself as a doctor, he first understood himself as a man of God. Black leaders today have forgotten about "the Rev" that comes before their names. They have forgotten who they were in God and chose to take a hold on being the activists for the black people. That's the only way Martin L. King made the difference that he made—he was God's man before he was ours.

CHAPTER 2:
THE GRAND HEADACHE

I will share my theoretical opinion because I believe in the "truth" foundation on which it originated. America's attitude toward people of color and other non-white people may be to keep them in the second class mindset. One of the reasons I feel this country is so weak is because the majority are not too fond of embracing a power other than their own. White America does not mind how rich a black person becomes as long as his wealth remains powerless. These extremely wealthy blacks are afraid to embrace their own people because they are afraid of losing their wealth. Wealthy blacks are aware that they have their fortune because of Mr. Whitey's hand. As they say, "don't bite the hand that feeds you."

Black America has little to do with the affairs of this country, such as a good sound piece of legislation. I say this because it is hard to get anything good for blacks out of committees. I believe that the blacks in Congress are there to keep the seats warm. In my opinion, blacks in Congress will be booted out if they actually try to do their jobs. Scooter

Libby was awarded amnesty after the big CIA leak. If a "certain lying VP aide" were black, they would have not given him time to put his shoes on before trying to throw him in prison. The message can't be anymore clear; look across the presidency and tell me if you find a black president.

Fortunately, we have a black man running for the White House, Barack Hussein Obama. Unfortunately, they are pressing him against his pastor of 20 years, Pastor J. Wright, who made such emotionally driven comments about America. They are calling for him to cut ties with his pastor, but in that case, all of black America needs to cut ties with white America. There are some Americans that would rather die than have a black as the commander-in-chief of this country. The question on Mr. Whitey's mind is, "Why doesn't Obama run for president in Kenya?" You know what, that question is probably the most sensible question to ask Obama.

African people don't know what it is like to be discriminated against because of being black. The only form of discrimination they know well is being discriminated against because of being poor. Africa is predominately black; there we are the majority. I'm hoping blacks with a grave understanding in their hearts realize that we don't have to lose who we are to be black in America. There are many countries in Africa where we can bring a great deal of ourselves and our education to help change some governmental flaws. As educated as Obama is, I am shocked at his closed mind. Even so, I will vote for him just to satisfy my own curiosity for his "change" agenda. This is nothing more than a hope that blacks will come out of their co-dependent mindsets. Like anything else it will take time, dedication, and hard work along with fearlessness.

We don't have to be hateful or disgusted. We have the

ability to love not only each other but others. This is something that we have that the so-called "majority" of this country has never seemed to attain. If we are indeed hated because our color is different, than we should be glad; that means our color causes that green-eyed Devil that's better known as jealousy to show our power and beauty through its ignorance. I hope you understood that I say this to the shame of the white's and not too much for our glory. It has been better for us to be the least of nations so the power of God can be shown through our nation. This message is not a *blame* message. It is a *take responsibility* message to black America for black Africa. Have we come too far to change, or are we stuck in co-dependency? Have we altogether become unprofitable? We are a people of faith; we are the royal priesthood the chosen and set apart people. Then why do we not want to acknowledge the power of God? Why do we not understand that our faith can be used for greater things than houses, cars, and money. This message is not limited to just blacks but any people that have destructive co-dependent mindsets. I focus on black people because these are my nation, they are mine. They are near and dear to my heart. I can understand how Moses felt when he came to know who he was. He saw how his people were being treated and it hurt and deeply troubled him. This kind of hurt makes you move, it makes you do something. It's that same hurt that made our Martin L. King march and our beloved Rosa Parks sit down. That same hurt is what moves our black leaders to do something other than sit there and watch. That same hurt moved me to write this book but I must admit nothing hurt me more than what they did to Emmitt Till. Emmitt was a 14 yr old child that was brutally murdered and thrown into the Mississippi river. They did this to him because he whistled at a white woman.

I have been doing self-observations and self-studies on

racism for 15 years, and I feel I may be on the right path concerning the causes of racism. There is no better way to find the answer than to look through the eyes of spiritual truth. We as people of faith need to believe God for the impossible things. Without God we can do nothing; I believe there are only a few that share this hurt and if there are many that share this, then they need to "move."

I love America, but I love her with a hard and bitter love. I don't love what it is doing to my people. I don't love the leadership because they are too small-minded to lead this country. Our leaders, making their foreign policies, are creating more terrorism against this country. At least blacks can't be blamed for the corruption of foreign policy! Need a hint, NFTA; the way I see it, since white America wants their country, let them die for it. Too many blacks are fighting for this country when they are not even wanted in this country. Blacks put up with being labeled by the white majority. Blacks also put up with the constant reminder of who is in charge. We deal with this on our jobs and even in typical daily affairs such as going to the grocery store; we deal with dirty looks because we have to shop at the same grocer as whites. So far as the military is concerned; I will never encourage a black person to join the military, although I did join the military, and I did like it for the most part. I probably would be in Iraq if I had not received a Section 2. Thank God for Section 2! You know, I would not mind supporting service in the military for our blacks if we were treated with the same respect and equality that whites treated themselves with. We know that will never happen! We have been shut down, shut out and shot, and hung for that matter. So I say leave the Majority to its own wars and let the minorities have prayer because they tend to be rich in faith. The bottom line: let's love one another blacks and whites, but I believe the whites will love us better sitting at our own table. True love is fearless and bears the truth and his name is Yahweh. Let us blacks be true to ourselves. We are not built to act or to assimilate into white people and the same goes for whites and any other color or race. As for the whites or the majority, the bullying technique is failing fast. America has bullied other nations so much that the bullied are getting weary of it. Those nations have turned to terrorism to hurt this country. I believe that the solution to terrorism is to let them rule their own countries, and the U.S. should show decency in dealing with the way others choose to run their countries. If we know we are dependent on foreign countries for their goods, than we should make a foreign policy that will help encourage well-being for each other's economies and have no tolerance for bullying of any kind from anyone. The country that wants to break that policy will be subject to sanctions. I'm not big on politics but it does not take a degree from Harvard to screw in a light bulb. Underhanded dealings are a seed that will have devastating consequences as we saw on 9/11. That faithful day black and white realized that they both were sheep in the lion's den.

CHAPTER 3:
BLACK SUPPORT OF AFRICA

I do get to exercise the luxury of the freedom of speech for something other than pointless rhetoric. The following chapter is my own little idea of how to support diverse countries in Africa. I know black people are going to say it is the craziest thing they have ever read, but please, entertain me for the moment.

Hopefully, we will be able to change things for blacks and whites for the better of both races. You know what they say: "It is better for feuding couples to live apart rather than together." That statement may hold true for the terrible relationship between blacks and whites. Some of you may question how in the world that could ever happen. Well, just because our two races are better off apart does not mean we don't need each other. For those who would like to go "home," we should make it possible. Various people should come together and start a home-going fund for those blacks that wish to relocate to Africa. I know not all blacks are up to this kind of a challenge, but there are many that are. I bet American taxpayers would love to give for that cause.

Our highly educated blacks would be great in undeveloped countries in Africa. They could bring their expertise to the people and start business that would lead to jobs. Black America could bring much needed relief to those children that live in the slums of Africa. After all, it does not make sense for the same people who are trying to kill our people to help feed them. Our business blacks that are at the peak of the corporate ladder should be more open-minded to such a thing. This would beat marching any day of the week. I do believe at this point we can begin to develop new visions for our black people. For many blacks no matter their wealth or lack, this is inconceivable, because many blacks don't acknowledge Africa. True enough; many blacks are stuck in co-dependency so deep that they don't even realize that they are free to think for themselves and their people. This mindset has to be pulled out by the roots in order for us to even begin to dream or have visions.

It is predicted in the next 40 years the Latinos will become the new majority in America. Now, black America, where in the world do you think this kind of change is going to leave us and our children? If we do not begin to think for the sake of our children, it is likely they will wind up working in agriculture. It is a possibility if we do not get out of our state of stupid. Fear and laziness are the greatest enemies of black people. The only way to conquer fear is to get educated. Learn how to make something from nothing, but make something meaningful, not rap music. We can start by accepting that Africa is our passage-way home. We need to make it our business to learn as much as we can about Africa so we do not have to be afraid of the unknown. We are like children that are lost in the wilderness and can't find their way home. New Orleans victims are an example of this. They're scattered across this country, while at the same time, the government is selling their properties right out from under them. This is the same way we are displaced as a nation. It is a sad truth that blacks completely have turned their backs on Africa and have disowned her. Our nation is like a sheep that has left the flock to go and embrace a wolf.

I have had many tell me I should join a certain black faction. To them I say, "What for? They are fighting battles that they will keep losing." This faction is like a group of mouthy, powerless politicians who are only interested in personal gain. Is that a harsh thing to say America? Maybe it is, but the proof is in their bottom line. They just want Mr. Whitey to like us and treat us fairly so we can have the same interest rates as white people, so we can have a piece of the American pie. This faction needs to understand the fight is not about our skin color but about our co-dependency on whites. If you ask them to let go of the white man's pant leg, they will turn around and look you square in the eye and say, "Now what are we going to do for food?"

I'm not saying we don't need white people—we do in a responsible way. It seems we may have lost our great faith in God to be our provider. We cannot talk hateful about Africa because that's where blacks sojourned, so to talk down on Africa to ourselves or in front of white people makes us look really bad as a people. Be thankful for America, but let's take what we have learned from her and make it work for our own people. Believe it or not, whites want us to be proud of who we are, but they want us to do it from Africa. God made many different kinds of people—he also made many different kinds of animals—but that does not mean that it is good for them to share the same territory.

CHAPTER 4:
SPIRITUAL THEORY
ON RACISM

Have we as humanity fallen so far that we have never attained the ability to accept that there is a God? How else can we explain why an entire race of people has become so gullible? This race has become so off track that the Devil has purposed to use them every conceivable way he can. I believe all races have fallen victim to this deceit, but there is no race of people that has been more taken by this evil than the Caucasian race.

When you have a people collectively, that can slaughter innocent men, women and children, then count it as a hard day's work, you are dealing with more than just insane people. Has any one of us sat down and really thought about it? This race of people has slaughtered blacks with no mercy just like Hitler had no mercy on the Jews. These acts in my opinion are comparable to the way demons act in hell. A devil does not feel remorse, nor does he have compassion on the littlest people. They make available pictures of blacks being hanged, like it is something to be so proud of. I have seen pictures of my people hanged from trees. I've even seen a picture of a black man being set on fire while he was still alive. They stood around looking at him as if he were some kind of decoration for the ground. Say what you will America, that's just a little disturbing to me. They could even take a small black child and kill him as if he were some wild animal. We only can imagine what they did to the poor Native Americans. As for us, the answer to these atrocities can be found in the Book of Deuteronomy chapter 28.

We have got to realize that in some people racism is not just about color of skin, it's about much more. Let's not forget about the Colfax Massacre on April 13, 1873 in Colfax Louisiana. There fell contested elections for Governor and local offices. Whites armed with rifles and small cannons overpowered freedmen and state militia (mostly black men) trying to control the parish courthouse. White republican officeholders were not attacked. The majority of the freedmen were killed after they surrendered. Estimates of the dead vary, but the military report in 1875, identified the deaths of 3 white men and 105 black men. And 15-20 bodies of unidentified black men were recovered from the Red River. Some of these people believe that only white people have a right to even exist. Regardless, this has become, for a lack of a better word, "sick." We know that the Devil has to choose earthen vessels with which to cause trouble. The Devil is the prince of this world, and it's safe to assume we know what people he likes to use most. I'm not saying the Devil does not use other races but not on the scale as the Caucasians. Theoretically speaking, there had to be an entry point for the Devil to pollute this people with this unspeakable evil.

"Caucasian" is a term used to describe a particular race. It originated from the 19th century study of craniology. It was derived from the region of the Caucasus Mountains. The

18th century German philosopher Christophe Meiners first named the concept of the Caucasian race, but the term was more popularized in the 19th century. It came under the name Verietas Caucasia, by the German scientist and naturalist Johann Friedrich Blumenbach who borrowed the name Caucasian from Meiners. Blumenbach based classification of the Caucasian race primarily on skull features. Blumenbach believed that the Caucasian race was the oldest race of man and the first variety of human kind. He also believed the region of Mt. Caucasus, both because of its neighborhood and especially its southern slope, produced the most beautiful race of men. His main reference is the Georgian. He believes this because of physiological reasons. In 1915 French diplomat Arthur De Gobineau believed the white race had their first settlement in the Caucasus region.

It is believed that the origin of whites came from a Greek myth god named Prometheus. He was known for his wily intelligence and for stealing fire from Zeus and giving it to the mortals for their use.

Zeus was also a Greek myth god who imprisoned many titans who opposed him, like Prometheus, who wound up banished outside the civilized world inhabited by the Colchins. The Greeks considered the Colchins a barbaric people, whom in my opinion, obviously were a bad influence on the Caucasians. The Messiah resisted the Devil's temptations of worldly power, but it seems like someone else took the bait. I mean, this is the only logical answer for how an entire race of people can be capable of such horrific acts. We need to pray for Caucasians that God will set their hearts free from such a sick disease that can only come from the Devil.

Listen, I'm not beating up on the white people because all white people are not this way. There is a great deal of white people who couldn't care less what color you are and what you have, but the number of them are so small, you have no idea who they are. Let me tell you, if you ever get one of the clean whites as a friend, you have made friends with a wonderful human being. Clean whites are very beautiful people and are full of sunshine and love. They will lay their lives on the line for you. The same goes for a white who gets a clean black person whom does not live in the shadow of history. This kind of black is just as beautiful and loyal as a person can become. The truth is, we all can be clean from the trap that the Devil has set for us. We do not have to be hateful and resentful toward one another.

There are also spiritual lessons to learn. For starters, we must understand that some things we hold of great price in this realm of life are trash in the spiritual. They include material objects, self superiority, and anything else that would make us think we are smarter than God. By no means should we hate each other, I cannot express that enough. The whites do need to be aware that their race is targeted by the Devil, and he will use them to spread his message of pride, hate, and arrogance. To the blacks and the self made Jews, we should not be too bent out of shape about the past perils our people had to endure. I believe facing these perils was for the saving of our souls later. Remember, after they have killed the body, they can do nothing else. Our people suffered so that we could have a closer walk with God, and so we would not be consumed by pride and arrogance which are diseases of the soul. Rather, for those that have given themselves over to the power of darkness, they should be afraid, for the indignation of God is reserved for this kind of evil.

The trick of the Devil is this: he has convinced the whites that having white skin is of some value or importance. For instance, Christophe Meiners first defined the Caucasian race "a pure race, whose racial purity was exemplified by the venerated ancient Germans." Although he considered some Europeans as impure "dirty whites" and "Mongolians," who consist of everyone else, Meiners did not include the Jews as Caucasians and ascribed them a permanently degenerate nature. When the truth of it is, the body is just a dust suit for the spirit.

The vast majority of whites are Catholic which means they have a profound but deadly understanding of God. The Devil knows this, so he has devised a plan to keep the whites idol, so they will never grow to the perfect love and maturity in God. The Devil has caused the blacks to hate the whites because they are all we see, but behind the scene the Devil is at work. If there was any power in white skin, surely it would have been made of something other than dirt. The good news: there are many whites that have been set free from the Devil's darkness. The only effective way to tell if you have a clean white person is if you make him angry and he does not use racial slurs, or demeans you because of your color, than it's probably safe to assume you have a good friend. Tell me this America, if I'm so full of it, than how many white children have lately been murdered simply because they are white, or how many whites have been killed simply because they are white? I rest my case!

Now, can you believe that if a white person saw a black child drowning and there was no one else around, the white person would probably let that child drown? I know you want to know how I could say something like that. I have had it happen to me. I was about 14 years old when a friend and I decided to go swimming. Mind you, we were not perfect swimmers. My friend went a little too far in the deep end, and he could not swim. Since I was a better swimmer than he was, I went to pull him back over to the shallow end. The next thing I knew, he was on top of my head using me as a floating device. He absolutely panicked! We both were in serious trouble. The whole time this was going on there was a white boy sitting alongside the pool watching the whole thing unfold and did not lift one finger to help. God gets the credit for why my friend and I are still alive today. Yes, America, the white boy could swim, and he swam like a professional swimmer. Just because that particular white person was a complete and total idiot, I'm not angry with him, but unless he changes, he is already condemned.

Whether you are black or white, if you yield yourself to the Devil, you give him permission to put his hands on your children. This is why we are facing some issues with young children today we never thought we would see. There is a middle ground that blacks and whites can meet in peace, but the truth has got to stop being swept under the rug. Whites tend to teach their children that anything that isn't white isn't right, when in fact whites probably are the most homicidal people on the face of the earth. The violence of whites is now not so much physical, although when it is physical, it is brutish. Their violence is to attack the root of a people. For blacks, it's our families, and for foreigners it's their governments. Don't get me wrong, I'm not a racist, but humanity has a serious problem that needs to be fixed. If this problem is not fixed, the guilty parties involved will have an eternity of contempt to look forward to, and down there you cannot tell the Jew from the Gentile.

Rachelle Mbuangi

CHAPTER 5:
SPIRITUAL THEORY ON
CAUCASIAN HOMICIDE

My theological conclusion of why whites have been allowed to be at the zenith of humanity is as follows: I've noticed during my observation that they possess characteristics that are almost on a superhuman level. This is very impressive to say the least. One of their characteristics is their perseverance. It takes commitment to colonize a place and bring it from nothing to something. That in itself is a breathtaking feat. They endured great hardships, including times when the infant colonies were facing extinction due to illnesses and battle. Nevertheless, they succeeded.

They also have a competitive side, a side that turns into homicide from time to time. This homicidal characteristic has unfortunately led to the enslavement and vicious murders of blacks. This competitive homicidal characteristic did not come from the God who created them. Although it sounds elementary to say the Devil made them do it, it is a possibility. The grand majority of the race is corrupted by this evil. This corruption of their spirits has rolled down through the generations. This same corruption of spirit is found in many other races on an individual level, but the whites have everyone else beat "hands down," so to speak. Regardless of this evil, they have been permitted to oversee the day-to-day affairs of men. They have been given power they have never learned to use properly. They would never have been given this power had Zion not turned from "the Lord our God". Whether that power comes from a good source is another question. Their perseverance and fearlessness have exceeded that of many other races in my opinion.

On the other hand, they do have insecurities that they hide using ominous tactics. One commonly used is intimidation. They also have an ability to win over a person's trust and confidence, while hiding their crossed fingers behind their backs. They are very tactical people and are masters of deception, becoming this way through heavy education.

The whites have known the weaknesses of blacks for many decades. They know if they can keep us sinning against Yahweh we will never inherit our promise. Black people are opportunists, well, the younger generations are. Some blacks tend to favor short, quick paths to success, while whites, on the other hand, are not afraid of long, hard work and sacrifice. Unsurprisingly, blacks hate to lose anything. Whites tend to look at their next step forward, regardless of loss, while blacks tend to keep looking behind themselves to their demise. Whites have managed to bypass us and excel over us because they know our weaknesses, such as our lack of education. Every man-made house has its weak spots, and the spot of the whites is for blacks to be highly educated in godly things with liberty being the base. That's why they hate the Jews so much—because of their education and their ability to excel at anything. Whites know that if blacks ever grasp this concept, blacks will begin to rise up out of their oppression. Whites love for us to keep our focus on the fact that our people were kept in slavery, murdered and discriminated against. So long as we keep our focus on trying to make them feel guilty, we won't have time to focus on the steps that are in front of us that will inevitably lead us to mentally evolving. The enslavement of our people was one of Gods curses on his people for their disobedience. Whites are only puppets for Yahweh to carry out his will. And after that, he will turn around and judge our enemies for their mistreatment of his people. He wants to show us he is "GOD".

Another reason I believe whites scramble to keep blacks under their cloud of oppression is because they believe that if blacks get power over them, they will seek revenge. Whites are still hung up in the "Rahowa" mindsets. The truth is that blacks are not polluted on the same level as whites are when it comes to power. Blacks just want to live, enjoy life, and be happy and prosperous. Blacks are not "hell bent" on getting revenge for what whites have done. We leave that job to the God that created them. At the end of the day every man will go to his grave and the only thing that people will remember is how he or she died. Surprisingly, the way that you leave this world tells a short story about how you lived in this world. It is no doubt discomforting over the level of insurmountable hatred that the so-called "majority" is projecting worldwide.

It's been said, by various sources, that white American aid workers were injecting African children with the HIV virus. There is a chance that this is fictitious, but I bet it's closer to the truth than many realize. As with any evil, it's like fire: if you don't put it down it will consume you. These soldiers of the race war will fall on their own swords.

Whites really believe that being the same color as pork or poultry is an advantage. This is a classic deceit of the Devil; Satan himself deceives many into thinking he is an angel of light, not an angel of white. Color of skin is only limited to this realm of life. Being black or white or any color holds no candle to character. There are white fools and black fools. There are poor whites and poor blacks. The last statistic showed between blacks and whites on welfare whites have the highest percentage of welfare recipients –70%. So at least we are not number one in that vote. It had only to be the Devil who persuaded them to believe that they are the superior race. Only cancer has a need to spread without good reason.

There will always be a root deep in the hearts of black people to keep them in touch with the past perils of our ancestors. I do believe the worst thing we can do is to let our ancestors die in vain. We need to have a new vision and a new dream. We need not be afraid of sacrifice, as long as we have our God whom can save us from the fiery darts of the Devil. Only through him can we wage a victorious and peaceful war against the Devil and his chosen. Remember, the battle belongs to the Lord. There are vessels fit for honor and vessels for dishonor. Which one will you be? The fear of man is a snag, and I do believe we have been snagged long enough, but we are not snagged worse than our white neighbors. If anything we should pray earnestly for ourselves and for the whites. They do not realize that their evil acts will curse their own children. We can recall the readings about what God did to Sodom and Gomorrah.

Furthermore, blacks have yet to learn the art of unity. It is something that our nation has fumbled the ball on indefinitely. We need each other to make the biggest difference. Notice how white people will lift their own people up even if the person is not the best qualified. To them if another's skin is white, that's enough. We need to adapt that same loyalty for one another. We need to understand that we have the same rights as they have. We need not be afraid of them or angry with them or resentful toward them. Rather, we need to look upon them in compassion and pity because they are a people that have been taken by life and money. They measure their worth by what they have, and if that's all they are then we really have nothing to be angry or resentful about.

The road that lies behind us shows us the times when we as blacks had nothing, but we were plentiful in faith, hope and strong character. Thus we are wealthier than they will ever be or have been. Again, all whites are not this way. Some are actually human underneath their skin. Blacks know how to face adversity pretty well. We know how to face the impossible without having to self-terminate because of the lack of material wealth. The next time a white person tries to display his worthless superiority, be humble in your spirit and let him satisfy himself, because that's all he has to keep himself feeling important. At the end of the day that white person has no rest in his own soul and he is tormented daily. Even knowing what I know concerning the place of black people in this temporary chapter of life, if I had the choice to be black or white, I would choose to be black. It is better to have black skin with fullness of spirit in the faith than to have white skin and be full of great darkness and contempt.

This book is not written to put down whites but to expose the Devil on a much higher level. If you are white, and if at the end of this book you feel that you have been enlightened, than there is hope. If you are black, and if at the end of this book you still feel like white people owes you something, than you are a part of the problem and not the solution. May peace follow all races as we walk toward the end of this vapor we call life. Let us not come to the end and find we have run the faith race in vain.

CHAPTER 6:
THE FALL OUT FROM MONEY

I doubt if anyone in the black community, except for those that are of the household of faith, will wait for the door to swing the other way. The whites will eventually drag humanity into the ground just as we are seeing them do in our government. There is no foundation built of sand that will not give way.

I've noticed black business owners suffer the effects of being kept out of the privileged circle. I know because I am a business owner. You can be a black business owner as long as you stay in your place as "negro." As long as you don't do as well or better than them (whites), your prosperity is tolerable. If you begin to excel past them, they will do what they can to bring you down. To what avail do they do these pointless displays of power? This same planet they are trying to dominate will turn around and destroy them and many around the world.

Why do we hold so firm to the foolish and unlearned things of life? Why have we allowed the Devil to creep in and lead us captive by something as insignificant as a tree? Don't tell me you do not understand the tree concept; we make money with wood. I have to remind you, since this country has made money its new God, strange things are transpiring. We wage war; we sue our own children and mothers in court; we self-terminate; we mislead sheep with false doctrine; and we murder our own children—all because of a tree. It sounds pretty dumb when you use the prime ingredient to make money, as the primary name for our currency. With all of this evil in the sight of the living God, where is our fear? We have become taken by our own hearts imagination. We stake our claims as if we are going to live forever. This sadness plagues my heart and tickles my mind. I'm one who loves people no matter what race they are. For those of us who have a true love for people, we often suffer from a broken heart.

As you have read, I put whites under very hard scrutiny. I do so because I—as a human being—expect better from them. I know some bigots would probably ask, "Who do you think you are to say something like that?" Well, I decided to say what so many others want to say, but are too afraid. It was God who created us all and allowed whites to be in their positions. As a believer of my Heavenly Father, and the Messiah I do expect better from us.

Rachelle Mbuangi

CHAPTER 7:
THE MOVE THAT
CHANGED THE WORLD

There was a great event that changed the world, both economically and agriculturally. This event largely in part may be the motivation for the Caucasian race viewing blacks as profoundly lazy. Compared to this event, they may be right. This event is called the Columbian Exchange. This event impacted ecology as well as culture. The term is used to describe the enormous wide spread exchange of plants, animals, foods, human populations, including slaves, communicable diseases and ideas between the Eastern and Western hemispheres that occurred after 1492. This great event began a new revolution in the Americas and in Europe.

The Columbian Exchange affected almost every society on earth, bringing destructive diseases that depopulated many cultures and also circulated a wide variety of new crops. This exchange of plants and animals transformed European, American, African and Asian ways of life. This exchange led to 50 million Europeans coming to the Americas. To give an idea of how big this event was, consider before this exchange occurred: there were no oranges in Florida, no bananas in Ecuador, no paprika in Hungary, no tomatoes in Italy, no pineapples in Hawaii, no rubber trees in Africa, no cattle in Texas, no burros in Mexico, no chili peppers in Thailand and India, no cigarettes in France and no chocolate in Switzerland. Even the dandelion was brought to America by Europeans for use as an herb. The Columbian Exchange changed everything. Now, there is no positive without the negative. Diseases ravaged populations around the world because of this exchange.

When I was a child and I heard that white people were nasty people, I thought it was a figure of speech, but it is true. True enough no two races are alike, but it seems every race around the world has in some way made great sacrifices for themselves and their children so that they can have a decent quality of life. The shame for the Black Americans, in my opinion, is we are too comfortable with being taken care of. As I mentioned earlier, we seem to enjoy being called the minority as long as we get to eat. We don't even try to make a real sacrificial effort to pave our own way apart from our white neighbors. The civil rights movement was needed in order for future black generations to dream. Is this how we are going to repay Martin Luther King Jr. and the other elite black activists? How about the first black slaves who were brought here fresh out of Africa—what honor do they get? How do you think they may have felt being forced to work for complete and total strangers and never being able to see their loved ones again? When will we make history for our own, so we will know the meaning of being responsible for our own race as a whole?

One thing about the Caucasians in theory is that they are very eager to help those who help themselves. They don't hamper the true effort of those who sincerely want to make a difference. On the other hand, they despise those who only look for a handout, and those who believe the rest of the world owes them something. The Caucasians don't owe us anything except to help us become a self-efficient race, being they interfered with the nature of the African/Hebrew. There were some Africans who sold other Africans to the whites. These are the blacks that should have been prosecuted and thrown in prison for the rest of their lives. Unfortunately, Africa had no democracy at that time. How can we as a black race have any dignity by allowing ourselves to be trampled down? As long as we don't have to lose anything, it seems we are perfectly fine with being stepped on.

I don't condone violence in any form or fashion, but there is much we can learn from the Haitians. The Haitian Revolution (1791-1804) was the most successful of the many African slave rebellions in the Western Hemisphere. It established Haiti as a free black republic, the first of its kind. By means of this revolution, Africans and people of African ancestry freed themselves from French colonization and from slavery. As for us today, that kind of fighting is not necessary. We have it much easier today than they had it back then. Largely, African countries today are going through stability issues. There are countries in Africa where people are surviving and living well below the "American" poverty line. Through a random selection, Nairobi, Kenya is the city I chose for a topic of discussion. Nairobi is the most populous city in East Africa, with an estimated population of between 4 and 5 million, according to the 1999 census. Nairobi is now one of the most prominent cities in Africa, politically and financially. It is home to many companies and organizations. Nairobi is established as a hub for business and culture.

In my opinion, many Black Americans think of Africa as

a vast forest, with blacks living in the trees and amongst the wild life. This is true for the country "folk" in Africa, but there are more Africans living in the city than in the country. Largely, the reason for this misperception by Black Americans is the projections we see of Africa on television. These projections are to attract tourism, but they are not a good depiction of life in Africa. We hardly ever see any media documentation of big cities in the African continent. There are many Africans that are doing financially better than many blacks in America. We owe it to ourselves to take time to study our place of origin. I firmly believe you will find that the apple never falls too far from the tree. We have much in common with our African brothers and sisters.

We should turn our focus on those of our African people living in slums. In Nairobi, we can find many areas where we have much to offer our people. For instance, Kibera is one of Africa's largest slums. Most Kenyans in Nairobi are poor and live in these slums. This is due largely to urbanization, poor town planning and the unavailability of loans for low income earners. Now, this is where it gets a little heavy; it's time for us to sacrifice. Black America has turned its back on changing things for our people. We have left the job to the Caucasian, who is doing nothing more than exploiting our starving children for profit. Some of these organizations may be legitimate, but none are honest. Sadly, if the Caucasians don't do anything for our own people, nothing will get done.

Rachelle Mbuangi

CHAPTER 8:
POLITICS IN COLOR

So far as I'm concerned political America is nothing more than bigot agenda. True enough, we have some whites in office that are what we can call "decent." I doubt if we have any whites that are 100% "bigot clean." If we do, they are the better for politics. Bigotry in government has been there since the first Congress. What do you believe was on Theodore Roosevelt's mind when he decided to name the congressional assembly building the "White House"? It does not speak unity for all to me. President Harrison was the first to put electricity in the White House but then was too afraid to touch the light switch for fear of retaliation from opposing others. Now, at least our country's leaders are not afraid to turn the lights on!

I'm surprised with all the division in the White House. There was one president that I thought was halfway decent. His name was President Taft—you know—the one that was good friends with Roosevelt. Anyway, they were friends until they started running against each other for the presidency. Well, like any presidential run between candidates the mudslinging got pretty bad. The mud slinging got so bad between Taft and Roosevelt that Taft was moved to tears because he could not believe how bad things had gotten between himself and Roosevelt. Anyhow, Taft won the mudslinging contest, only to be conquered by the stresses of being president. Taft also later went on to become Chief Justice at which he excelled.

What I liked about Taft was his insight into future presidents abusing executive power. This reminds me of a Bush abusing executive power (and it's not the bush Bill Clinton didn't inhale). Listen, this is only my opinion, others may feel Taft was a complete disappointment. We are all entitled to our opinion. Even so, Taft will never be worse than the president who fumbled the ball during the Hurricane Katrina crisis. Here's that Bush again (and I don't mean the beer, either). This hurricane came to reveal the hidden imaginations of the conservative majority; others think God sent it as punishment to the sinful city. Regardless, it came to uncover the truth about what is in the hearts of this country's leaders. There are lessons to be learned from this storm; what are we going to do for the next catastrophe that wants to reveal something?

Anyway, back to politics, remember when the whites got their independence from the British on July 4, 1776? There is a trick question that has tickled my brain for many years: which of the 3 deaths was more honorable? A: Being killed against your will over your own property. B: Voluntarily dying for stolen goods that did not belong to you. C: Being slaughtered for no reason. I know that sounds a little blunt, but it is a serious question.

There are many controversial things that I have written in this book. These things may inadvertently entice many people to "think," but they do it every day on talk radio with their bigotry "hanging out," so what's the difference? I do write this book out of concern for the direction of both the black and white races. In addition, we all know when we operate out of fairness of mind we want to make the best possible decisions for those involved.

Even though I'm not into politics, I like to watch CSPAN. It's sometimes fun to watch these college graduates better known as senators rant and rave at each other like children. Almost more than not, the only true way this nation will change is to face the truth and stop hiding from it. I say this because I saw a serious unwillingness for Congress to come up with comprehensive immigration reform. To appease myself, I came up with my own version of their reform.

Well, here is my version of their immigration reform. For starters, immigrants illegally in the country for less than 9 years must return to their countries. If they are immigrants married to Americans for a period of two years, no criminal background and have at least one child, the American may file for his spouse to obtain residency. If the immigrant has been in the country for 10 years working, has no criminal record and learns English, he should obtain the legal right to work in the U.S. if he pays a 3,000 dollar fine, serves 8 years probation and pays a flat tax of 2,500 dollars during the probation period.

Children of those immigrants that were here for less than 9 years will be kept in an orphanage-type facility funded by the immigrant population. These children must be 5 years or older to remain in the U.S. If they are younger they must return with their parents to their country of origin. This is the sovereign right of the U.S., with some humanity. Immigrants of all types, no matter the country, will pay a 2.5% AGI to fund the orphanage for immigrant children.

This money will pay for the building, food, education, child-care workers and medical cost that the children will incur.

Immigrants, whether legal or illegal, must forfeit benefits reserved for American-born citizens, although immigrants will have the right to invest in the stock markets to make a way for their retirement. These restrictions do not apply to immigrants married to American-born citizens. Employers who really feel the need for cheap labor must sign an affidavit of support for the immigrant worker and his immediate family. The employer will be responsible for housing, food, cost of living, health insurance and anything else related to daily life needs. If an immigrant commits a crime other than minor traffic violations he will be deported. Immigrants with school age children must pay for their children's lunches at school no matter the income. This does not apply to immigrants married to American-born citizens.

The immigrant funding program will be overseen by our government appointed faction. Our taxpayers will not be burdened with the responsibility of supporting immigrants, since the immigrant population is so big it should be self-sustaining. Also, taxpayers should not be burdened with supporting immigrant children under the age of 18 years, with both parents being citizens outside the country. Immigrants must pay taxes no matter what the income. For example, if the immigrant only makes 2,500 dollars annually than he can at least pay 250 dollars in taxes. Payment plans will be afforded to the immigrants as a tax benefit. Deportation for the immigrants that are here less than 9 years will happen after the construction of the orphanage for the children is complete. Immigrants with no children will deport immediately.

As for the border, the reality is that we cannot stop these people from crossing the desert to get to the border. So what we should do is build a smooth concrete wall about 20 feet tall along the entire 1700 miles of border. We then leave an opening the size of a typical front door. This opening will lead to the inside of the border security building. We will allow humanitarians to provide food and water inside of the building. If these immigrants have come to such a desperate situation that will drive them across the desert to face possible death, than they deserve to come here and be the backbone of America's agriculture.

These immigrants will be identified by some sort of identification badge, worn around their necks at all times. These immigrants will be our guest workers. Because there will be so many wanting to enter, we will have to work out a seasonal cycle plan with the Mexican government. This will allow different immigrants who brave across the hot desert to have an opportunity to earn money so they can feed their families back in Mexico. This will be for Mexican immigrants only. Our taxpayers would supply our agriculture department with the funding to afford bunkers and to house the certain number of immigrants needed by each agriculture location. Mexico should be responsible for a controlled path for immigrants coming across the desert. There should be water available for every two hours of walking along this controlled path.

For the 9 year deports, they will be allowed 30 days visitation with their school age children that are in the U.S. These visitors will come 50 at a time every 12 months. They will wear an alarm bracelet that will be set on a timer. When it is time to leave, this timer will emit a loud noise at the end of the 30 days. The bracelet cannot be removed unless by the immigration authorities or local law enforcement. If it is tampered with, it will emit a loud noise. This noise can only be turned off by immigration security or law enforcement.

Hey, it may not be a perfect reform but it's something. I told you I'm not big on politics, but I do have a big heart for people. When you have a genuine love and care for human beings, no matter what race they are, you can come up with humane ways to deal with the most difficult situations that affect the lives of people. Of course, to most of the vast majority of bigots, this won't work either. Unless we treat illegal immigrants like the settlers treated the Indians, they won't be satisfied. Furthermore, our ability to unite with whites will only be done through complete and total disregard for color. Unfortunately, ignorance has gone unabated for far too long. Maybe those that have constructive criticism about this book could be a part of the solution instead of the problem. Listen, you don't have to take my word for it. Just look at the facts in history. Those of us that are searing from the constant heat of oppression need to exercise the freedom of speech in a manner that will propagate progress.

Rachelle Mbuangi

CHAPTER 9:
THE RELIGIOUS OBSERVATION

Let us just be truthful about this religious road. There are white churches as well as black churches, and there is the Church of Scientology. These diverse churches are sprinkled across the great U.S. I went to an all-white church a couple of times. My family and I were the only blacks there. Caucasian people believe in giving an attentive ear to what the preacher is saying. The whites do worship, but it is not to the tune of entertainment. They worship with respect to God and they worship with order. They honor God like he is the true King, but nobody knows how to praise God better than the Devil. Now, whether this manner of service is true to heart is another issue, because some of these same whites sitting in church on Sunday practice discrimination Monday through Friday. I never read in the Bible where it said only the conservatives will enter the Kingdom of Heaven. We need not talk about the Scientology Church at all!

On the other hand, blacks are more colorful in their service to God. Blacks tend to love the traditional ways of service. The way they were taught on the plantation by "massa". They tend to love gossip, back biting, tale bearing and with the same mouth and feet running, and screaming and passing out to show their spiritual attainment. No, I'm not judging my people; we have all fallen short of the glory of God. I've never gone to a Hispanic church, but I'm sure the basic church theme is the same. I'm pretty sure every church has its imperfections, but we need always remember as fellow laborers in the gospel, that the Devil knows the power that we have with God. It's a shame we don't.

I'm going to help just a little in our true devotion to the powerful God we serve. If we are to grow in a pure heart for hearing God, than we must learn how to be mindful of God. We must learn the importance of solitude so that we can hear from God. Yes, I do love God; that's why I have made it my business to learn more about how to treat the King of Kings and Lord of Lords. God is much more than some genie granting peoples wants and desires. We have to have a genuine love for him. When you truly love God, you are not going to serve him for only what you can get out of him. You will have a desire to want to be close to him, just as a child wants to feel the love and warmth of his parents. The child does not always just want things from his parents; he wants to feel the bond between himself and his parents. We should have the same desire toward our God. We should learn how to meditate on that bond so it can grow stronger, and so that we can become more efficient at striving for that blamelessness that is in Christ Jesus.

I'm going to share with you an excerpt from a book that I read concerning the importance of silence in the faith. This excerpt comes from the insight of Ignatius of Antioch and it reads:

"Indeed, it is better to keep silent and be, than to make

fluent professions and not be. No doubt it is a fine thing to instruct others, but only if the speaker practices what he preaches. One such Teacher there is: He who 'spake the word, and it was done' (Ps 33,9), and what he achieved even by his silences was well worthy of the Father. A man who has truly mastered the utterances of Jesus will also be able to apprehend his silence, and thus reach full spiritual maturity, so that his own words have the force of actions and his silences the significance of speech."

Now, if we as God-loving people can master our mouths and the internal gate to our spirit, we can know what it feels like to have a real experience with God, instead of feeling really good emotionally and tying our emotions to an experience with God. Let us find the power that we have with God so we can be more effective in our daily walk with him.

CHAPTER 10:
THE CHILD
REARING CONTRAST

It's known that whites tend to pass down not only their cuture but their life experiences to their children—as well as their ignorance. I was in a hospital lobby gift shop one particular day, along with my two children who were 4 and 5 years old. In walked two little Caucasian girls; they may have been around the ages of 7 and 5 years old. My little girl is very friendly and she said hello to the little girls. Those girls gave my daughter the most hateful stare I've ever seen in a child-to-child encounter. My little girl looked up at me with a sad expression on her face. I told my daughter, "Some people are not very nice." The oldest little girl of the two looked at me with that famous I Never look on her face I tend to believe whites don't realize that passing this kind of hatred down to their kids will only lead to more destructive leadership of this country. The settlers worked so hard to steal this country from the Indians, so please don't destroy America with your racism.

Blacks on the other hand don't teach their children

anything except how to fight. Blacks need to sit down and talk to their children about money: how to earn it, how to save it and how to invest it. Believe me, whites teach this to their children.

Some whites teach their children about how "bad" black people are. Whites might need to stop teaching their children that kind of rhetoric, especially to their little girls. Their little girls grow up and become attracted to that "bad boy" image. That's why when white girls go after black guys; they go after the ones with criminal backgrounds. The whites should tell their children how good and educated blacks are so their girls will think that black guys are nerds. Then their girls will go marry the white guys with a criminal background.

Black children tend to think that being who they are is bad. The way to help break that cycle in our black children is to stop buying them white baby dolls and white action figures. Stop buying those video games that portray black people as violent and criminal. Instead, buy them games like *Monopoly*. This will at least give them a basic idea about real estate. I know America, *Monopoly* is old, but it can still serve a good purpose. Black people need to wake up and smell the stock market because it has a great effect on their every day financial lives. This book is not going be a long drawn-out book of open-ended facts. Rather, it is to the point.

Rachelle Mbuangi

CHAPTER 11:
THE UN-CONFIDENCE

My latest thought stems from the confidence and dignity that I see in white people daily. Like it or not, they can have it, because their people fought for it. My ultimate plan is to compel blacks to see their demise in the U.S. Although, the U.S. is a great country, it will be nothing more than a privileged prison for black people. Blacks will never be able to straighten their backs, hold their heads up and walk with pride that is made strong through willful sacrifice. We will always be somewhat comparable to leeches in the face of white America. Our black leaders know we need to stand and do something, but they have no idea what it is. They are shooting darts in the dark.

Our great Martin Luther King actually knew what needed to be done for his time, through God's guidance. Therefore, Martin Luther King's target was given to him by God, and that's why he hit his target "dead on." This is an excerpt from a MLK JR. sermon against the Vietnam War:

"As if the weight of such a commitment to the life and health of America were not enough, another burden of responsibility was placed upon me in 1954. And I cannot forget the Nobel Prize for Peace was also a commission to work harder than I had ever worked before for the brotherhood of man. This is a calling that takes me beyond national allegiances, but even if it were not present I would yet have to live with the meaning of my commitment to the ministry of Jesus Christ. To me the relationship of this ministry to the making of peace is so obvious that I sometimes marvel at those who ask me why I'm speaking against the war. Could it be that they do not know that the good news was meant for all men—for the communist and capitalist, for their children and ours, for black and for whites, for revolutionary and conservative? Have they forgotten that my ministry is in obedience to the one who loved his enemies so fully that he died for them."

Martin's sacrifice was his life. He knew there was a possibility that he would be killed, but that did not stop him from doing God's will. Our black leaders today are well-respected throughout black America, yet the sadness of the matter is, they have been sucked under by capitalism. In simpler terms, they have been overcome by their love for money and popularity. They also lack the ability to fight racism because they have not taken the time to really sit down and understand the white man's position on it. The Bible says, "With all thy getting wisdom, get understanding."

That situation with radio talk man, Don Imus, really upset me. I don't believe he should have lost his job. In my opinion, he made that statement simply because he really believed that was the way blacks communicated with one another. I believe that he really thought it was viewed as something positive we say to our black women. He is not to blame for that misunderstanding; it's our sorry excuse for music we call rap, which I will talk about later. Meanwhile, he should get his job back. It was not right to fire him for a misunderstanding. Black people need to stop playing the victim even when they know a situation was just a misunderstanding and not a gesture of hatred. We need to learn the difference! Don't get me wrong, most of the time these situations are gestures of hatred, but I do believe this man was just one of those misunderstandings that happened in the open.

CHAPTER 12:
THE HIP-HOP ERA

This is an era that I know all too well. First, let me start by saying I'm satisfied that our young men and women have a talent to sing. Now, I said sing; what I hear now is young men and women that can talk really fast and make the words rhyme. The language of hip-hop and R&B has changed dramatically over the many generations. Each generation is worse than the one before. On top of that, we have the nerve to call it a culture. It's more like a cultural nightmare.

This so-called "hip-hop culture" is the leading cause of destructive mindsets in our black teenage boys and girls. Now, even the black hip-hop artists know it is an ominous thing to become a millionaire off of being able to rhyme words and talk really fast. Okay, what I am trying to say is "have we lost our minds"! How on earth have we allowed ourselves to become puppets? Hip-hop lures young black minds from being involved with making national decisions to better lives for blacks in this great country. Instead, this sad embarrassment called hip-hop culture has caused our children to believe that going to prison, "catching a charge" and just being plain brutal is the good life. Hip-hop artists don't teach that going to college and becoming engineers, architects and doctors, of which rips off the health care system, is the way to the "bling, bling." Instead, they teach the way to the bling is to sell large amounts of drugs and to take young black women and horde them into prostitution, so that the pimp can make money off of her.

Our black female R&B singers are an utter disgrace to our black women as a whole. They teach our young black girls that the way to get the bling is to use their bodies. These singers are showing parts of their bodies that should be hidden. They are teaching our girls that to have a promising future as a female in a good relationship, the size of her bum (bum is a nice foreign word for butt) is the deciding factor. Now, you have Hillary Clinton running for president. She is a very accomplished woman and her bum is flat. So please, all of you influential hip-hop females, stop shaking yourselves all over the place. Learn to use your brains to get your bling, because that big, fat bum one day will go south and turn into cellulite.

You hip-hop guys and girls need to be able to do something other than talk & rhyme. You girls need to learn something other than using your pretty voices and bodies. To be honest, you're making all these millions and millions of powerless dollars. Meanwhile, the rest of your race is being mistreated, starving to death and being poorly educated. You could learn a thing or two from Oprah; build a school somewhere for black children to learn something; for example, build a school for them to learn who they were before slavery. I'm not knocking your talents, but do something else besides helping to destroy your own people. There are a lot of whites who listen to hip-hop but very few are destroyed by it.

Rachelle Mbuangi

CHAPTER 13:
THE ASSIMILATION

This aspect of America fosters a great deal of the infectious disease called racism. The first thing we should understand is that the ways of peace, love and temperance, and self-control coupled with patience and understanding, are not the ways of white people. These are the ways of God. Largely, whites have managed to live by these principles so that their way of life can be worth preserving. I believe young blacks try their best to live the opposite of these principles because they grow up thinking these are "white people ways." Mankind in general is too evil and wayward to think up such divine principles. It was God that gave us these principles to live by whether we are black or white. This is the foundation of the assimilation theory.

I have seen trees with strong roots begin the growth process as one tree and then split into two different trees, yet they are still bound by the same root. Well, that's pretty close to the same way assimilation is. We all must adhere to the basic principles that foster peaceful living between neighbors, while at the same time living different paths of life.

As we take a closer look at this assimilation, its bottom line is to make life in America more favorable to the white citizens. This is why whites are kept in the more privileged circles of America. Now, whites really intended for blacks to forget who they are and where they are from. This is why blacks are called "African Americans" and "minority." White America is so sore at Latinos because Latinos bring their culture with them. Latinos refuse to assimilate into the more white characteristics of America. They would much rather stay in touch with who they are. Unlike Black Americans, Latinos believe that unity is strength. This has a great deal to do with why blacks receive no respect from anyone, because we are the most divided race on earth. Latinos have a belief and confidence in themselves that can be seen outwardly in everything they do. They believe the same thing a white person can do, they can do it too.

Black America, we can all adhere to the basic principles of life given to us by God. At the same time, we can be true to who we are. Our people were raised in captivity; there is no way we will know who we are; unless we retrieve what was stolen from us at the beginning. I do have my little concerns, however. We need to stop trying to live like white people if we are not willing to do what they did, to get what they have. There are some blacks that are inside the privileged circle, but whites don't make it easy for us to get there. Even still, the door is open to anyone (Yes, they at least had to open the door, or risk being called racists).

The Supreme Court ruled to stop sending our children to schools based on race. Now, this means that the poor and geographically challenged will be horded into one district and the privileged kids into another district. You know what that means; the low income children will probably end up with the "teacher rejects," the teachers who couldn't care less whether your children learn, just as long as they get that paycheck.

There are solutions. Parents that can afford it, put your children in private school. I'm not saying this will have a significant impact on the number of children finishing school, but it is a bit higher than those that attend public schools. For the parents that cannot afford private school, be involved with your child's education.

Here is another solution: *get off your bum, black America.* Go to work. Do something other than sitting and watching. I know you vote democrat but live by republican principles. No, I don't mean become crooks; earn an honest living. Get out there and make your own way, black America, and stop waiting for someone else to do it for you. I know there are some of you that would not do anything, even if there was a wolf behind you. God gave us all a talent and the resources by which to use that talent. Find out what yours is and use it, and I'm not referring to rap. Be mindful black America; use your talent so that you can escape the death grip America has on you. A lazy person will never have anything! Learn from the white people; just don't go bungee jumping or skydiving. There is no need to be resentful toward whites. If we can learn to do everything the opposite of "sit down," we will be able to at least be on the right path, for a better future for our kids. The bible refers to America as the land of our captivity, and those that took us captive as our enemies. Do not do as they do black America, go not in the ways of them that seek your life, because your life here is given you for a prey.

CHAPTER 14:
RHETORIC OPINION ON ISLAM

Unfortunately, Islam is the center of much controversy. Whether we like it or not, the radical believers of Islam will only grow worse. They bore their way through the holes in our so-called "civilized" societies. They have one leg over on us, so to speak, because we are bound by the parameters of civilized living; we have to walk right, talk right and dress right.

I have observed how America's attitude toward Islamic extremists went from *Oh! It's just another religious belief to Oh my God. These people are crazy.* The evidence shows that they believe in something that they are ready to die for. We cannot defeat them on a military level, so the only way in my view to beat them is to put aside being heavily civilized. No, for goodness sake, I don't mean for our boys to blow themselves up. The truth is, I would like to give my opinion on how I think we should fight them, but I believe that the war is a disaster. With so much corruption worldwide in governments, Islamic "fascists" will find a way to creep through the cracks and impose their beliefs on innocent people somewhere. Wherever this happens, I'm sure it will lead to the mass slaughter of believing Christians. Hey, it could happen!

I know dealing with these extremists is emotionally draining on families with loved ones serving overseas. This feeling is probably comparable to that gnat buzzing in your ear on a hot summer's day. Eventually, the fire of their evil will be put out in obscure darkness, but by the time that happens many of us probably will be dead—of natural causes of course.

I'm weary of Muslims throwing the Qur'an around like it's the only religion in the world. The Messiah is the King of Kings and Lord of Lords. No matter what goes on, the Messiah is the Holy Lamb of Yahweh. He will be the only divine one standing after the dust from this religious war clears. No matter how many of our Christian brothers and sisters are killed at the hands of extremists, our God has already won and there has never been, nor will there ever be, a God like ours. He is the Alpha and Omega, the beginning and the end, praise is to Yahweh forever and ever. Amen.

Look, I know you probably think this is religious dogma, but it needed to be said. In my opinion, it's an outrage and a disgrace for the people of God to lie down, while the Holy Bible has to share its seat as the founding book with some other Bible. I know the bible was used deceitfully in the founding of America. This is why at some point we need to be thinking about leaving before the judgment of Yahweh falls. Now that I got that out of my system, I feel much better.

Rachelle Mbuangi

CHAPTER 15:
INNOCENCE LOST TO
POLITICS / SAVED BY RELIGION

Let me start this off by asking, *have we as a country gone completely insane?* How in the world are we allowing young children, even babies, to be sexually, physically and mentally abused? Now, before I move on let me make one thing clear about disciplining our children: there is a fine line between abuse and using the "good old fashioned spanking." Listen America, we can very much protect our kids from abuse, but don't infringe on the rights of respectable parents to physically discipline their children. Because of some of these ridiculous laws that basically allow children to divorce parents and take away the parent's right of being a parent, they have caused an epidemic of disobedience in children. It is a slap in the face to those of us who love our children. Then in the same breath, we turn around and ask why a child killed his parents or why children are so out of control. To make it simple, don't try to pass laws to stop parents from physically disciplining their children.

I will tell my children, "If you do something that warrants

a spanking and you decide to call the police, make sure you have your clothes packed so you can go home with the police." They are still my babies, but when they are in their mid-teens I will tell them. I will not have any children that I bore for nine long months telling me what they will and won't do in my house. Now, look America, I know you think that sounds a little harsh, but if we don't stand up and be parents the way we are supposed to and stop trying to be friends with our kids, we are going to have more kids killing their parents and committing senseless crimes.

We need to encourage fathers to have active, positive roles in the lives of their children. I feel in order for that to happen, we need to stop these power-driven women from using the laws that are meant to govern families in crises, as a weapon to keep fathers away from their children. These women should be thrown in jail for alienating fathers from their children.

Now that's out of the way, let's talk about our children falling victim to sexual predators. I'm going to put this as simple as possible: if Congress won't toughen laws on these predators, then we as loving parents and protectors of our children need to forget about whose black and white and organize to come up with an effective way to protect our children. As parents we need to get on the web, find out who our kids are talking to and look for signs of a possible predator. Then lure the individual to a location, and we the parents or group of parents, will be waiting at that spot and call the police once we have confirmation of the predator. Now, I call that an effective way to protect our children. I refuse to live like I'm powerless to protect my children from these kinds of people.

Parents, stop leaving your young children unattended for any period of time. Be careful whom you leave your sons and daughters with. I know all too well what it was like to be a child who was raped by an adult. I also know what it was like as a child to be molested by several different people over a period of 10 years. So I believe I earned the merits to have some say in protecting our children. If your child is a victim of rape or molestation, it most likely will have mental effects on the child in his or her adulthood. The good news is it can be overcome if you want to overcome. I have heard a lot of media coverage on white children that have been abducted or killed and not too much about any other race; let me just say it! We don't hear media coverage about black kids; I could get into the whole racist thing but I won't. The real color in this situation is green. If you have the money to pay for national attention, you can get it. If not, you don't get it. The truth of the matter is, we must do better when it comes to protecting our children. While we are on the subject of children, though, let me turn focus to something else.

There is something that I have been seeing on television for many years and I still believe it's just another ploy to undermine black families. It is a charity organization, which shall remain nameless. Now, I don't know if it's just me, but considering how many years this has been going on, shouldn't these children be living in mansions by now? My question is: why are they just using the same tired phrase "Help us help the children"? Common sense would tell any logical thinking person to better help those children we need to help the parents. The parents are dying at an alarming rate of AIDS, so shouldn't that be the focus, to try and prolong the lives of these parents so they can raise their children? If the organization could change its phrase to, "Help us help the parents provide for the children," the organization probably would not get one red dime, or should I say one white dime! Everyone knows those children are black.

I saw on television the same organization on location in India. (You know, to help those children who look like white kids with a tan.) The Indian children were eating strawberries and watermelon. They also had spoons to eat with. Now, I saw black children eating with spoons too on some occasions, I'm trying to be fair here. Anyway, these children even had what looked like a nice eating area with green tile walls and fans to keep them cool. I did not see the families torn apart by AIDS and HIV. Do you know that AIDS has wiped out entire African communities? Well, let me get back to the compare and contrast of Indian and African children. The little black children were eating what looked like mush. I am pretty sure the mush was full of nutrients, but it did not look appetizing. I want to know why the little black children weren't given strawberries and watermelon. It could be that they may have eaten those fruits; I may not have been able to see it. I just wanted to put what I saw from television on to paper. I'm not sure about the minor details that may have caused these dramatic differences between the treatment of the little children but I'm sure I will find some. It may be the governments of those countries cause such problems so the little children receive improper help. We know that racism is alive and well everywhere.

I remember hearing a candidate in the primaries say that the problem of racism could be addressed through economics. I know this is a little off topic and he may be right, but I say, "What a load of crap." Pardon my language, but racism exists in the hearts of men. Unless the heart is purified and cleansed by the power of God, racism will still be there no matter how much consumption is available. The only thing we will end up with is a bunch of "full bigots" and a bunch of "full, uneducated blacks who don't have a clue." Hey, I could be wrong; let's see if his theory is right.

If you doubt that God has the cure, just read the Bible. Either we can submit and let God change us the easy way, or take the hard way. Knowing America, we will take the hard way. Black America, it is ok to want to be more economically inclined, but let's do it for the right reasons, not as a cure for racism. We have got to stop using Cold War methods to curb racism. We must be a people pure in heart, a people that walks in love and forgiveness, and only then will we see clear how to cure racism. Listen, even if you are not a Christian read the book of Zephaniah and you will learn God's hard way, to teach us how we are supposed to conduct ourselves in this world.

CHAPTER 16:
THE LANGUAGE
OF CHRISTIANITY

I do respect that everyone is not religious, so if you are one of those people, I ask respectfully for you to bear with me on this view. I have respect for the Christian leaders in the faith. I have been hearing a great deal about the coming of our Lord Jesus Christ. That is good news and that is something to get ready for. I have a great concern for the sheep. I'm concerned that their preparation for the Lord's Coming is slightly misguided. Now listen, I'm not undermining our anointed preachers of the Gospel, but my spirit is gravely concerned.

I'm going to share another passage of a book that I study for my spiritual growth. It is the writings of Basil, a Holy man of God. He is more widely known amongst the Catholics. Here is what Basil wrote:

"Then, once the obstacles, disturbances and occupations which are usual in human life are accepted, he is not able to maintain that which is greater than all and more precious: the memory of God. Once this is driven out and excluded from the soul, all divine joy and gladness is lost. His capacity to find delight in the Lord is diminished and he no longer experiences the sweetness of the divine promises… So he comes into the neglect and forgetfulness of the divine judgments and falls into a habit of counting them as unimportant. There is no state worse or more destructive than this."

Truly, we do not know the day or the hour of our Lord's return; we can collectively agree on that. I have heard from some of our fellow laborers in the Lord that we are the generation to see the return of our Christ. While this may have been revealed by the Holy Spirit to some, we are not preparing the sheep as we should. Jesus said, "No one knows the day nor hour of his return." He did tell us of certain things that this generation will endure before his coming, but because there is no easy way to discuss this, I won't. I will instead suggest for you to read it yourself.

Remember, read a Bible you can understand. Everyone cannot understand the King James Version. My advice for those people is to try reading the New International Version. Trying reading: Matt 24:1-31; Luke 21:7-28&32-36; Zephaniah 1:2-3&14-17-2:1-3; Rev. 7:9 & 13-17. I'm not forcing religion on anyone so please don't be offended. You don't have to read these Scriptures. This is just for the household of faith and for those that want to love God.

Anyway, if you have taken the time to read these Scriptures you are probably wondering, *WHAT?* Based only on the belief that we will be the generation to see the coming of Christ, we must inevitably endure through the great tribulation. The great tribulation will occur during and after the indignation. Now, when God says, "I will wipe the tears off of their faces, they shall hunger nor thirst anymore, nor shall the sun smite them nor any heat forever…" I just have

Rachelle Mbuangi

a hard time believing he is talking about your heavy exercise workout that causes you to thirst for a nice, cold glass of orange juice. As well, when you're driving down the freeway and you say, "I sure am hungry. Let me stop at a fast food restaurant." I don't know about you, but that does not sound like a plausible hunger or thirst to me. I believe you know where I'm going with this; don't misunderstand me—no one knows the full mind of God.

Respectively speaking to the Sheppard's of our Lord the Messiah, if indeed we are the generation to see our Lord come, then we shall also witness the greatest act of our God in all of human history. We will witness his indignation on the entire world. Well, it is an easy thing to say; we don't know who that generation will be, if so led by the Holy Spirit, nor do we know the coming of our Lord Jesus Christ. Collectively, let us be ready in case we are that generation.

It is believed that we will be raptured away before the indignation period, but as you may have read, the elect will be here to see the great act of God. How could the rapture come and take us away if the elect are going to remain here to face the tribulation?

"Immediately after the distress of those days "the sun will be darkened, and the moon will not give its light; the stars will fall from the sky, and the heavenly bodies will be shaken. At that time, the sign of the son of man will appear in the sky, and all the nations of the earth will mourn. They will see the son of man coming on the clouds of the sky, with power and great glory. And he will send his angels with a loud trumpet call, and they will gather his elect from the four winds of the earth (Matt 24:29-31).

That does not sound like a nuclear fall out to me although it can happen in the mist of the panic. I know there will be some that will refer to this as a religious pastime. You know, it's not that I didn't know this little book would raise so much "talk," but these things needed to be said. So far as the Bible is concerned, you don't have to believe me. Read it for yourself and let God lead you accordingly. Hopefully you let this view find you in a peaceful mind.

Rachelle Mbuangi

CHAPTER 17:
DARFUR

This particular view is dedicated to the many innocent men, women and children that have been murdered and assaulted in the Darfur region. This is a very sensitive subject to me, being I am a person who has suffered verbal, mental, emotional, as well as physical abuse as a young child. You better believe it when I tell you that God witnesses the good and the evil. I believe I can safely say we know that our beloved U.S. knows a little something about the horrors in Darfur. At least that's what my gut says. I am going to try to speak for those that have been permanently silenced in Darfur. Now, I want to know where these so-called "Janjuweed" are getting their weapons from. Why can't we give the innocent victims of Darfur weapons to defend themselves? We gave the Iraqi people weapons to defend themselves against the insurgents. The last I heard about the effort to protect Darfur was that they would send more troops into the region, except the troops had to come from other African countries. I do believe we have a double standard situation. Truly, I am at a loss for words; this is something beyond me.

Now do you believe what I said about the Devil using a certain people?

U.S. troops have been deployed to fight a war that really is senseless. These troops could have been deployed to fight for a real cause, like saving the lives of innocent children in Darfur, not for some dictator country. Little girls as young as 5 and 7 years old have been brutally raped. Entire families have been slaughtered like animals for no reason at all. If they are suffering this because diverse governments believe these people are hiding Bin Laden, why kill children, mothers and fathers? They are killing people that have nothing to do with politics or Bin Laden.

They should just go after the government leaders. Leave the village people alone; our troops would have more respect for laying their lives down to fight for people who cannot defend themselves. I do believe if we had any casualties, it would not be because our boys lost a fight with the Janjuweed. The casualties probably would come from overeating, not by the hands of a people that are running around with weapons they barely know how to use. Instead, our troops are fighting in Iraq with over 3,400 casualties.

Listen, I do not know the facts surrounding the Darfur horrors, but I have a feeling our great country knows. What kind of people are we to close our eyes to the cries of the children of Darfur? *OH YEA! I forgot they're black.* How could I have been so foolish to forget such an important ingredient? Bigot America would not hear of their precious white soldiers dying for the likes of blacks. Yea, I said that ugly truth; I know some bigots think I should be punished for such a statement. I'm saying things that a mother of a murdered 5 year old probably wants to say. If terrorists can have weapons to shoot down American choppers and kill our soldiers, why can't the villagers of Darfur have weapons of some kind to defend their young children and families?

I guarantee you, if you have anyone trying to aggressively enter the home of an American with the intent to do harm, that American will have the right to bear arms and defend his home. At least, that's the way it used to be. So please, tell me; why can't Darfur villagers have the right to protect themselves? Okay, here is the ugly truth: the people of Darfur are black and others in the world couldn't really care less. Now let's picture these people white.

This chapter is dedicated to the beautiful children, fathers and mothers who have lost their lives or have been brutally abused in the Darfur Region.—You are remembered.

CHAPTER 18:
ANIMAL RIGHTS
VS HUMAN RIGHTS

This view is written due to the black football player that lost his livelihood because of dog fighting. He shall remain nameless. I am an animal lover and I do not support the mistreatment of animals. I believe that this individual was wrong, but I do not believe his long-term freedom should be taken from him, all because of what he has been charged with.

I feel his punishment should fit the crime. I feel that the football player should never be able to own any kind of animal the rest of his life. If he is caught with any kind of animal, he should spend 90 days in jail. If he is caught again, then that's 5 years in jail. Look, I am not a judge, but I believe there is a way to handle this without taking this man's life from him. After all, we are just talking about animals. We as advocates for animals cannot allow our emotions to rule over good, sound judgment. The football player is a human being so he is supposed to be treated in higher esteem than any animal. I just believe that because the color of his skin is black, that's all the more reason to "stick it to him." Whether we like it or not, we must be mature in our love for animals, not outrageous. It is an outrageous thing to take this man from his family all because of the excessive love that animal rights activist have for animals.

I saw how the animal rights activists stood out in front of the court house with everything except a pick axe, ready to punish the football player. I want to know where these animal rights people were when they caught that pervert that killed little Jessica Lunsford. Where are they when these child predators are out murdering the littlest citizens of America? Instead, they would much rather send a man to prison because of animals fighting. These are the outrageous people who pervert the love and care we are supposed to give every living creature. So I ask you—what is more important —to convict someone for punching a dog or for murdering a child?

Rachelle Mbuangi

CHAPTER 19:
THE CAUCASIAN ENEMY

For many centuries the Caucasians have believed that the other so-called "inferior" races are their enemy. At least that's my opinion, but it is hardly without evidence. This was exhibited during the slaughters and massacres of the indigenous people and black slaves. Even the very act of colonizing prompts the basis of my opinion. These people allowed their paranoia to get the best of them. Had they taken their knowledge, shared it with other societies and helped the weak to become a self-sustaining society, the rest of the world would probably have been happy to make them the headship of humanity. They could have gained everything that they have today through honor and respect. Instead, they felt the only way to get to the headship was through theft and violence tinged with brutality. Fortunately, the rest of the world wants to fire them as the headship of humanity because of their barbaric behavior. Whether my opinion holds merit or not is irrelevant in this age.

Their enemy has always been their own minds. They have ultimately destroyed themselves with their elementary theories created by people such as Christoph Meiners, Johann Friedrich Blumenbach, William Z. Ripley—author of *The Races of Europe*—and Benjamin Franklin, just to name a few. There is no dispute that these men were highly educated and great contributors to their race. Unfortunately, these theories caused some of the worst mindsets of their people. It seems with their educational accomplishments they learned nothing but how to devise mass discord. In my opinion, they made the whole of humanity on a humane level wax worse and worse. Consequently, they deteriorated any hope of the races coexisting as brothers instead of enemies (Not to mention those who came long before them). Most of the writers on theory came from Southern European civilizations and viewed Northern Europeans as barbarians. Somehow, I can't help but think the rest of us were stuck with the Northerners.

Benjamin Franklin proposed a clear distinction between white Europeans and "swarthy" Europeans. He stated that immigration to the newly born United States should favor the "white" Saxons and the Englishmen rather than the "swarthy" Germans. Franklin believed the white Europeans to be lovelier. Now, I must disagree. If he is going to turn this thing into a beauty pageant, I vote that the Arabic's are the most beautiful race of people. Don't get me wrong, my people aren't that bad looking, but we don't rank first in the pageant of the races.

Furthermore, I do ponder deeply when it comes to equality. By nature, the races are by no means equal, but this elementary awareness was exploited and turned into the great divider of races. The inequality of the races was meant to bond us together. It was meant for us to realize our need for each other. Instead, it has become the prime weapon of discord.

The Theory of the Nordic Race and the Theory of Aryanism were devastating blows for the Caucasian race. These theories followed the Caucasians for generations. The Nordic theory made its way into the U.S. through the primary spokesman for Nordicism, eugenicist Madison Grant. He wrote a book called *The Passing of the Great Race,* also known by its subtitle *The racial basis* of European history. This was highly influential among racial thinkers and government policy makers. Grant used this theory as justification for anti-immigration policies of the 1920s, arguing that immigrants from Southern and Eastern Europe represented a lesser type of European, and their numbers should not be increased. President Coolidge, for instance, signed the 1924 immigration act, restricting non-Northern European immigrants.

Now, by the 1930s criticism of the Nordicist model was growing in Britain and America. The British historian Arnold J. Toynbee, in a study of history (1934-1961), believed when a civilization responded to challenges, it grew. When a civilization failed to respond to a challenge, he noted, it entered its period of decline. In my opinion, this sounds a lot like Black America. He also argued that the most dynamic civilizations have arisen from racially mixed cultures. In Southern Europe the theory had always had less influence, for obvious reasons. However, the influence of Nordicism remained powerful in Germany. I will also have to agree with Mussolini, only concerning his statement that "Nothing will ever make me believe that biologically pure races can be shown to exist." Anyway, who cares if it did or did not! This same destructive Nordic theory helped drive Adolf Hitler into his madness, and writing the book *Mien Kempf.* Honestly, I never read Hitler's book because I can find better things to do with my eyes than read his rhetoric.

I believe we, as Black Americans, have got to let go of our painful history and move on. This problem is bigger than us and our demand for equality. This problem has come about from many great minds not knowing how to treat theory like a wild, untamed beast. There are some theories that are innocent enough in nature to be shared, but there are some that should never be spoken. History is made up of unending facts, which are nothing more than the acts of humanity striving for a more efficient way of surviving. Consequently, this leads to the nagging nature of us trying to explain things we know very little about, hence, "theory" is born.

Curiosity in itself is not a sin, but when you give curiosity a voice that has not been censored through the rigorous scrutiny of understanding, it inevitably turns homicidal. There are many of us that are guilty of spawning such grievous attempts of explaining the unknown, but the question is: could it be too late to do damage control?

There is a cry for brotherhood between the races that has yet to be pacified. Instead, the cry is being slowly silenced by war and brutality. As for those of us on a quest for justice, we may be guilty of the greatest injustices. Those of us on a quest for equality may be guilty of the greatest inequality. Destructive theories are vain attempts to explain the pieces that God used to put together his puzzle. We must embrace the maturity of accepting things that wish to remain unknown. God obviously likes diversity, but the Caucasians have taken it upon themselves to be the great judges of God's works. This will inevitably lead to the destruction of their works, and their children. Unless we turn from these unfruitful practices, we will hardly break the surface when it comes to coexisting together in America, which will lead to further mental bondage of black America. We are all created in the image of God. None of us are created by Greek myth gods. The idea of supremacy in any race is just "Devil's vanity."

In my attempt to explain the unknown reason why Caucasians have been endowed with knowledge that exceeds many other races (or the unknown ability to make applicable their unknown knowledge), they were given this ability as a gift from God. They were supposed to have used the gift as a means of uniting the races. Had they been obedient, they would have been placed at the head of humanity as a reward from God. Instead, they have taken God's kindness and used it for evil gain. The Caucasians have unleashed the Devil's arrogance upon themselves and are consumed by it. They have chosen to gain their headship through utter violence and brutish acts. This same sword they used to gain their uprising will be the same sword that will pierce them through with the unending slap of regret. Truth is the foundation of my theory; the act of the Caucasians is the same as breaking into your own house and stealing from yourself. Hopefully, there will be a great miracle that will at last bring brotherhood; without the derailment of worldwide economies through no fault of our own, but I believe that might be asking too much.

CHAPTER 20:
THE ENEMY OF
BLACK AMERICA

Just as our Caucasian neighbors, we are our own worst enemy. In my opinion, we are guilty of the greater "in-race" discrimination. How under the great heavens, do we think we can look to the white race and point our finger and call them inhumane? At least they take care of their own. They may have had a civil war, but at the end of the day, they are the keepers of their people.

We will disown each other over a piece of bread, and we will murder each other over 5 dollars. We mistreat each other in order to keep very minor job positions. When we become doctors and lawyers, the first people we kill and throw in prison are our own people. We are divided and destructive to our own people. Don't you believe we have suffered enough, without our own adding to the problem? We have no sense of loyalty to each other. Every chance we get to hurt one another, we take it. We have now become our own slave masters.

We do all these ungodly things to each other so we can score points with Mr. Whitey. These kinds of black people "make me sick," and they are the cancer of our race. If they believe that white people give them any respect for throwing their own people "under the bus," it is just the opposite. A white person views a black person in that state, of being a foolish and uneducated person, no matter the degrees earned. Even the white people view these kinds of blacks as disgraces to their own race. These black people are nothing more than worthless panderers. In my opinion, panhandlers have more respect than these kinds of cowardly blacks. Until we clean up our behavior toward each other, don't expect white America to respect our pleas for equality and any other proper treatment. Our people have forgotten what it is to unite and be loyal.

For instance, the Organization of African Unity (OAU) was established on May 25, 1963. It was disbanded on July 9, 2002, by its last chairperson, South African President Thabo Mbeki, and replaced by the African Union. The OAU's primary aims were to promote the unity and solidarity of the African states and act as a collective voice for the African continent. This was important to secure Africa's long-term economic and political future. Years of colonialism had weakened it socially, politically and economically. The OAU were dedicated to the eradication of all forms of colonialism, as when it was established, there were still a number of states that had not yet won their independence or were minority ruled. In my opinion, the "minority ruled" sounds just like Black America. Continuing, South Africa and Angola were two such countries that had not yet received their independence.

The OAU proposed two ways of ridding the continent of colonialism. Firstly, it would defend the interest of the independent countries and help to pursue those of still colonized ones. Secondly, it would remain neutral in terms of world affairs, preventing its members from being controlled by outside forces. The OAU also aimed to stay neutral in terms of global politics, which would prevent them from being controlled once again by outside powers. This was an especially important aim because of the Cold War. Other aims of the OAU were to ensure that all Africans enjoyed human rights, raise the living standards of all Africans and settle arguments without fighting but through peace and diplomatic negotiations. Soon after achieving independence, a number of African states expressed a growing desire for more unity within the continent. Not everyone agreed on how this unity could be achieved; however, two opinionated groups emerged in this respect.

The Casablanca bloc and the Monrovian bloc were the two groups that came about with ideas of how to attain the "unity." The Casablanca bloc was founded in 1961. It gathered other African countries such as Egypt and Ghana, led by Kwame Nkrumah. The Casablanca group merged into the OAU in 1963. The Monrovian bloc, led by Senghor of Senegal, felt unity should be achieved gradually through economic cooperation. There arose a dispute between the two groups which was solved when the Ethiopian Emperor, Haile Salassie I, invited the two groups to Addis Ababa where the OAU and its headquarters were subsequently established.

Of course any attempts the OAU made came under fire by the Westerners. This is nothing new; the Westerners have always tried to thwart anything that blacks try to do to liberate themselves. The OAU went through many obstacles and hardships to accomplish as much as they could. In some ways they were successful, and in my opinion it is no different than the colonizing efforts. No matter the hardship, keep moving forward.

I did not go into much talk about the civil rights movement in the Americas because this is something we know about as a race in America. I wanted to show other instances of unity by our people in Africa. Black America functions as an independent link. Until we take our place in the African chain of peace and justice for our people, we blacks in America will continue to function as a bound-minded minority in America. Black America has always been the missing link to all of Africa's freedom efforts.

I don't promote unity of our people as a way to prove anything to the whites, but to prove to ourselves that we can meet our white neighbors with dignity so that together along with the whites we can be responsible for our race instead of the whites being responsible for both our race and theirs. Only then can we coexist in America, and in the world, with peace and respect for each other's races, respect for our differences, and our need for each other.

Rachelle Mbuangi

THE CONCLUSION

Hopefully, there can be an amalgamation between the black and white races that will ultimately lead to the beginning of the end of pointless racism that began centuries ago. The apathetic torrents of Black Americans as a whole has inadvertently lead us astray as a race. It will take both blacks and whites to sit down together and draft a workable "race reform" to ensure the dignified coexistence for the two races.

"We must use time creatively and forever realize that the time is always hope to do great things".

—Martin Luther King

See 1stWorld Books at:

www.1stWorldPublishing.com

See our classic collection at:

www.1stWorldLibrary.com

Notes

Notes

Notes

Notes

Notes

Notes

Notes

Notes

Notes

Notes

Notes

Notes

www.ingramcontent.com/pod-product-compliance
Lightning Source LLC
LaVergne TN
LVHW091201080426
835509LV00006B/782